The Making of a Matriot

The Making of a Matriot

POETRY AND PROSE

1991–2003

Frances Payne Adler

RED HEN PRESS ● LOS ANGELES

THE MAKING OF A MATRIOT:
POETRY AND PROSE, 1991–2003

Cover photo of Helen Vandevere by Kira Carrillo Corser, © 1992
www.kiracorser.com

Photo of author by Richard Pitnick, © 2000

Book and cover design: Mark E. Cull

ISBN 1-888996-73-0
Library of Congress Catalog Card Number: 2003094586
Manufactured in Canada
Printed in Canada

Publication of this volume is made possible in part
through support by the California Arts Council

California
arts
Arts Council

and Friends of the Matriot.

Red Hen Press
www.redhen.org

First Edition

for Ali, Sara, Mike, Molly, Jake, and Sophie, as always,

and

for Lil and Jack
whose love for each other for 60 years has been my beacon

ACKNOWLEDGMENTS

I gratefully acknowledge and thank California State University Monterey Bay, the University of Wisconsin La Crosse, and the Helene Wurlitzer, March of Dimes, and James Irvine Foundations, for their generous support at critical times.

My thanks also to Kate Gale and Mark Cull of Red Hen Press for their belief in this book, and to Eloise Klein Healy and Peggy Shumaker for introducing me to Red Hen.

Thank you to Rina Benmayor, Jeanne DiGiovanni Howard, Bradley Zeve, Caroline Haskell, Devorah Stark, Marilyn Beck, and all the Friends of the Matriot, for their belief in the power of poetry and the struggle for justice, particularly in these challenging years. My gratitude.

A special thanks for their support and generous readings of portions of the manuscript to: Kira Carrillo Corser, Rhonda Hughes, Sandy Gillespie, Diana Garcia, Deb Busman, Adrienne Rich, Toi Derricotte, Dorianne Laux and Flight of the Mind, John Magerus, Federico Moramarco, Cecilia O'Leary, Tony Platt, Barbara London Rakov, Cynthia Hogue, Peg Cronin, Joyce Koskenmaki, Lynda Koolish, Jan Wagstaff, and Destiny Kinal.

Thank you to Yetta Gafko, Janie Silveria, Enid Irwin, Eddy Hogan, and Victor Henry, for research assistance; to Joe Larkin and CSUMB, for support of a crucial sabbatical; to Yolanda Perez, Stacy Kanne, and Erin McGee, for administrative assistance; and to Troy Challenger, Lark Simmons, and Arthur Simons, computer wizards. To Karuna Licht for her Big Sur writing retreat. To Anita Whitaker and Marianne Rowe, for their guidance and wisdom. To Nick Guzzi, for his enduring kindness. To Scott McGregor, who passed over the dreams. To my family who has inspired me to write, in joy, and in moments of despair. I thank you all.

Thank you also to Helen Vandevere, activist and mentor, who embodied the Matriot throughout the 20th century until her passing at the age of 94, and to Joyce and Judd for their steadfast work for peace and the environment.

And my gratitude, lastly, to Drs. Laura Esserman, Debu Tripathy, Brad Tamler, Stephanie Taylor, and Mindy Goldman, and to my breast cancer support group, and close friends and family, who carried me through it to the other side, and back to health. Without them, there would be no book.

❧

Grateful acknowledgment to Lucille Clifton, for permission to quote her in "Aftermath, September 11, 2001." To Dr. David Baker, for his quote in "The Great Lie;" To Kira Carrillo Corser, Maria Jesus Lopez and Lydia, for permission to tell their stories in "Disembodied," "Emergency Room, U.S.A." and "Lydia;" To Bettina Aptheker, for permission to quote her in "And How Is Your Heart?" To Cecilia Burciaga, for her translation of this indigenous Mexican greeting; And to Lee Blessing, for his play "Down The Road" on which the poem was based. For his gracious response, and permission.

Acknowledgment is made to the following publications in which these poems originally appeared: "Possibility," "Matriot," "Home, What It Costs" and "The Woman She Will Be," *poetrymagazine.com,* 2002; "The Breasted God," *Bridges: Calling Every Resource*, Eugene, OR. Volume 9, number 2. 2002; "The Voices Are Coming Up" and "A Call To Arms and Breast Cancer," *Cracking the Earth: A 25th Anniversary Anthology*, Corvallis, OR: Calyx Books, 2001; "Down The Road, The Voices" *Fiction International*, San Diego State Univ. Press, Fall 1999; "I Can" and "Rainwater, Re-Collecting," *Quarry West*, Univ. of California Santa Cruz, 1999; "The Fear That Doesn't," *The Progressive*, Madison, WI, May 1997; "Sam, Returns," *Poetry International*, San Diego State Univ. Press, Spring 1997; "Matriot," *The Progressive*, Madison, WI, May 1995; "The Hearing," published in an earlier version as "Wisconsin Works," *Capitol Times*, Madison, WI, November 1995; "Disembodied," *Healing*, Sacramento: Health Communication Research Institute, 1993; "Desaparecidos," *Raising the Tents*, Corvallis, OR: Calyx Books, 1993; "Blood Wash," *Pine Cone*, Pacific Grove, CA., March 1991.

❧

TABLE OF CONTENTS

INTRODUCTION

I. THAT SENSE OF URGENCY

II. HOME, WHAT IT COSTS

III. TURNING

IV. POSSIBILITY

V. WINTER GROUND

INTRODUCTION

THE WOMAN SHE WILL BE

the woman she will be
already has the woman she is
by the arm, she has been climbing her
down and up the gorge of two generations
losing the shape of the woman she
was constructed to be, becoming
the woman she is

the woman she will be
has been growing her these last
eighteen years, eighteen for *chai*,
for life, she has been sharpening her
eyes, educating her mouth, they have
become the deer bone of her spine

she has been growing her
for the coming evolution,
growing her to fluidity, long
languid lines, wide
love, arms thrown back,
moving belly open belly

I

That Sense of Urgency

How do you deal with the things you believe, live them not as theory, not even as emotion, but right on the line of action and effect and change? . . .

. . . That sense of writing at the edge, that sense of urgency, not because you choose it, but because you have to, that sense of survival – that's what the poem is out of . . .

— Audre Lorde

Reprinted with permission from *Sister Outsider* by Audre Lorde. Copyright © 1984 by Audre Lorde, The Crossing Press, a division of Ten Speed Press, Berkeley, CA. 94707, www.tenspeed.com

BLOOD WASH

Gulf war, 1991

Language is being laundered
in the west wing of the White House,
ordnances are being sortied.
Emptied of consequence.
Ordnances are no longer bombs,
they don't fall on flesh, they don't
tear open the skulls of women and men
rushing for shelter, they don't
empty the faces of children,
or crush bodies
carrying the small lives
of people like us

During the Gulf War in 1991, I was sitting at my desk and heard on the radio that our defense forces had invented a missile and named it the 'patriot.' That evening, I invented a word, asking myself, what does a 'matriot' look like?

Matriot (ma' - tri – at) *noun* 1. One who loves his or her country. 2. One who loves and protects the people of his or her country. 3. One who perceives national defense as health, education, and shelter of all people in his or her country, and the world.

© 1991 Frances Payne Adler

CRACKING OPEN

Mothers are dressing their children in bulletproof vests
to go to school, and the ceiling's on the floor.
The air has turned yellow, and my friend has to have a faucet
put in her stomach. The hinges between the ghost world and
the mortal one are cracking open.

Grey men in white suits play chess in the desert sand
with the hairless bodies of young women and men,
and decide they'll use their blood to run our cars —
it will be more honest. They'll sell real guns in toy stores.

1991

DISEMBODIED

for Kira

She wears the hang of a strong body,
walks six feet tall, size nine shoe,
holds the sky in her eyes.
Think you can defeat her?
You shall not have her, scorpion cancer
you shall not break her, you so-called healing
profession, healing industry, Medi-Cal, you supposed
healing arms of government

When the fine doctor tells her she has a
growth in your ovary she cries, remembering
her mother in the tub, and the scar
where her breast used to be, and when he says
Sorry his hand already on the door *I don't
take Medi-Cal* as if she doesn't deserve
his attention, as if she's not a person
and sick, she remembers *I loved to build forts
as a kid in Georgia, to dig tunnels, to furrow through the dirt*

And when the health insurance company, on embossed
letterhead, denies her insurance because she's sick, *you have a
pre-existing condition*, and when her government accuses her
of being sick, finds her guilty of not earning money,
requires her to call herself *indigent* to get health care
she's coming apart
she digs in, she's a fortress

When the gaping wound isn't healing,
her belly red raw fishflesh, she's screaming,
doctors scraping out infection without
anaesthetic *I forgot* as if she weren't
underneath *til you reminded me* Resist *I forgot
I could say no*

When the nightmare begins after the chemo
surreal to wake in the morning and see *hair*
everywhere, a pillow of hair, hair stuck to the walls,
stuck to the tub, stuck to my hands she's
crying, looking in the mirror and crying
she's coming apart

And when she's inside the toilet bowl
lying crying on the bathroom floor
retching four hours straight *This is the end*
I've reached the limit, I can't take anymore

And Keith down with her on the tiled floor
you're a fighter you're beating the cancer
you've got a lot to live for she kept remembering
her dream *I shall ride camels in Egypt*

1991

SHAPE

the shape of myself
a whole lotta noise

hairs along spokes of thin bone
jut at angles from my skin

lift them

my voice, blue as tin
hoarse from the vigilance

A Call To Arms and Breast Cancer

"What possible choices do most of us have in the air we breathe and the water we must drink?"

— Poet Audre Lorde, *A Burst of Light*, 1988

"Women with the highest exposure to the pesticide DDT, have four times the breast cancer risk. "

— Mary S. Wolff et al, *Journal of the National Cancer Institute* , 1993

"Our data do not support the hypothesis that exposure to DDT and PCBs increases the risk of breast cancer."

— David J. Hunter et al, *New England Journal of Medicine*, 1997

She grew up eating berries beans apples and peas and stuffed her bra with socks
She grew up eating grapes and greens, and on TV, breasts sold beer and cars and
musk perfume, jeans and jewels and junket tours, breasts and chests
and marketing plans, these golden globs, these silken globes

It sinks in early this thing with breasts, sinks into her
through apples coated with poison, poisons sliding down her throat
to her breasts, spreading like fingers along the milk route
Breast cancer, they tell her, we have to cut it off, they say, and they do,
and someone is singing *chest bust bosom tits chest bust bosom tits*

And they talk to her of fitting her for a fake one, No one will ever know, they say. *Know?*
she says, *I want everyone to know, I want to run up and up the streets
calling to women wearing prostheses, to yank them from their chests, to scatter
them on sidewalks, let everyone see us one-breasted women, millions of us*

How long are we going to go on killing women, she says, a chant, *how long*,
a prayer she murmurs as she slips in and out of sleep, *killing women*, her kidneys
giving out, her liver giving out, yellowing her skin, leaving her itchy, scratching
at her flesh, longing to get out of it and on to a world that makes some sense

And in her deathdream, breast cancer researchers collect the tossed prostheses,
trade them in like used bottles for gold from corporations who made millions
from all the cars from all the beer that breasts sold

CHLORDANE

DDT and chlordane belong to the same class of organochlorine pesticides.

"Prevention of breast cancer may require intervention at an early age . . ."

— Mary S. Wolff, *Environmental Health Perspectives*, 1995

green dust, green dust on the stairs, and the long-handled
wooden broom pushing the dust along, wafts of it in the air,
breathing it in all of us, up the stairs to the young classrooms,
all of us carrying our budding puberty, our gonads our
lunchboxes our ovaries our breasts, sucking it in, this
chlordane dust, this chlorinated insecticide
cracked from petroleum

"Comparison of Factory Prices of Prescription Drugs in U.S. and Canada,"
United States General Accounting Office, 1991

Drug	Prescribed for	Dose	Unit	Canada	U.S.	Diff.
Tylenol w/codeine	fever, pain	300/30 mgm	100 tabs	$ 3.32	19.38	484 %
Premarin	hormone repl.	.625 mgm	100	10.10	26.47	162%
Inderal	beta blocker: heart, bl. press	40 mgm	100	10.21	35.79	251%
Xanax	anxiety	.5 mgm	100	16.92	47.81	183%
Ativan	tranqilizer	1 mgm	100	6.16	49.43	702%
Naprosyn	arthritis	375 mgm	100	42.64	72.36	70%
Isordil	heart	10 mgm	100	1.63	17.41	967%

Raise the price
and praise the sick
who need our drugs
like water

Raise the price
and praise the children
who need our vaccines
like milk

Raise the price
and praise the elders —
medications
are their mother air

Raise the price
and praise the god
of demand and supply

Raise the price
and pass the champagne —
our stock is rising

1993

INDIGESTIBLE

greed has grown spiders,
crawled into everything,
become indigestible

workers in thick gloves
drive up, carry it all away,
all of our vomited spiderings

carry it all away in green
garbage trucks, the hydraulic
engines screeching and belching

Emergency Room, U.S.A.

Number of people in the U.S. with no health insurance in 1993: 37 million.

Many people rely on emergency departments for their health care.
Number of E.R. depts in Los Angeles County in 1988: 25. Number in 1993: 13.
Patients wait 6 hours in L.A; 15 in N.Y.

Maria Jesus Lopez waits. The hours grind her like metal into her wheelchair.
She crosses her legs, tugs her skirt, tries to hide her lost foot, says to Michael,
her great-grandson, *I miss my leg.* Her diabetes runs wild again like last year,
the cut that wouldn't heal, a foot blister that festered, turned black, slipped
slowly to gangrene. Had she had her own doctor, had she not, had she
not delayed coming here, the long wait, she gets tired, she didn't know,
the small sore, left untreated, might mean *amputate*

Down the freeway, at a different hospital, the man's cry — *Emergency* — spills
like a siren down halls clogged with waiting, past patients growing in rows
in their seats. He's yelling *Goddamn, give me something for my pain, can't you
give me something for my pain.* It's like this each time he comes here, he's
pacing, he's through waiting. Today, his head shaved, his camouflage
jacket hides a knife, three loaded guns, he paces the crowd, shoots
down three doctors. The patient pleads not guilty, one doctor
is near death, another sells the movie rights

The hospital, they add guard dogs, bulletproof screens, guards
round the clock, they install metal detectors

We're told this is not war

1993

THE GREAT LIE

"We delude ourselves into believing that medical care is available to everyone . . . Yes, people are dying because they can't get medical care. That's the truth. Don't sugar coat it. If we told the truth, then we could do something about it."

— Dr. David Baker, internist, public health,
Harbor-UCLA Medical Center, Los Angeles, 1993

The great lie hung itself like sheets
across the highway of faces speeding
to avoid it. It was a mess, a tangle of bodies
colliding with what was calling itself The Lie

It had a great PR committee, the old myths
announcing that *people who don't have health
insurance can just go to the emergency room
in the public hospital and get care.* And it

did such a sell job, that few suspected the pit
millions of people were falling into, city after
city, town after town, waiting for a pill, an X ray,
an antibiotic, small loving things

waiting hours, too sick to wait any more,
going home without care, but no matter.
The Lie was tired, its job description
obsolete. It was time

1993

"The number of Americans without health insurance climbed to 43.2 million last year, nearly one in six persons."

— Universal Health Care Action Network, 1998

Los Desaparecidos

*Estimates of people experiencing homelessness in the U.S in a given year
vary from 2.3 to 8 million, according to 1994–2001 studies.*

Like the mothers of Plaza de Mayo,
I can't put out the fire of disappearing.
On Fifth Avenue, next door to the Guild Theatre,
the man who blankets his child with newspaper,
sleeps in the crawl space of an apartment building.
He turns his face from the blade of light
thrown by patrons opening the theatre door.
They don't see him.
The woman whose feet ulcer from walking the night
on Washington Avenue hurries behind a wall.
In a house on La Mesa Boulevard,
a young girl who won't eat
sharpens her bones the color of fine blue china,
crawls under the tombstone pages of a fashion magazine.
On Ocean Beach Boulevard, 7-11 shoppers
see an old man with three coats stalling death,
sleeping on the heat exhaust
of an ice-making machine. In Argentina
and El Salvador, uniformed men
in jungles and in office buildings might laugh
at the fine way we mask mutilation. No death squads,
no white handprint warnings on doorways here.
No lye poured over bodies to make bones vanish.
In my city the desaparecidos obligingly
make themselves disappear.

1984

LYDIA

Lydia, standing outside, waiting to shower
at Rachel's Center for Women. It is not
what she expected, she says, living on the streets.
Sometimes sleeping on the floor in an abandoned
tire factory on Tenth Avenue, with three hundred
people in one room. Some on newspapers spread
thin to cut the cold, some on thin mattresses, all
on thin soup. It is not what she expected. It is visible,
this hunger she fights. For all those years she lived
in El Cajon, wore Calvin Klein slacks, drove her kids
to baseball, she could have been any one of us.
For all those years she blurred her husband's insults
with Valium, hunger was what happened just before
dinner. And when he left her, hunger, though she told
no one, was what happened when she couldn't find
herself in the mirror. Hunger all those years she was
draining slowly out like sawdust trailing from the doll
her daughter once cried for her to fix. Once, she too
had a doll, during the war. Lydia, born in Krupp,
Germany, down the street from the munitions factory.
She remembers getting dressed, not undressed,
to go to bed, ready to run from the bombardments.
Playing war with her doll, protecting her from shells.
Taking her brother in hand, knocking on doors for
bread. It is not, she says, so different living on the streets.
She knows this war. It was the bombardments in El
Cajon she couldn't see.

1984

MATRIOT

Helen Vandevere, born 1904

There's not much that's important at my age
except making the world a better place.
What would *I* do?
I say we damn well better
get out on the streets again.
Everyone has to put their hand to the wheel
and get out and get off their butt
like in the sixties. We had compassion then,
and we've lost it. It breaks my heart.
I've lived through two depressions,
two of them. Everyone at that time
was just sick about the way things were,
just like now, only it's worse now.
I see things falling apart —
People, living on the streets.
Children, beaten in their homes.
Sick people without health care.
Imagine this, in a country
that spends so much on the war machine.
I'd spend the money on health instead.
I'd see that children are born healthy
and make sure they stayed that way.
All children no matter what age.
I'd clean the air, the water. I'd take away
all that polluting shit they put on vegetables.
I'd promote the use of sun, sea, and wind
for natural energy. I'd save the forests,
especially the redwoods. I'd ban firearms.
I'd take away every nuclear device man to man.
No more wars, ever. *Now* we're talking health.
How are we going to pay for all this?
No one ever says we don't have enough
money to go to war. No one ever says
we don't have money for national defense.
This is national defense.

1992

II

HOME, WHAT IT COSTS

Do you hear the shifting/of the ground? How it moves . . .

— Sandy Gillespie

THE FEAR THAT DOESN'T

For Bessie Weisman Plonsky

Let me tell you a story. I had moved, a few years ago, from California to La Crosse, Wisconsin, to a big old house on 15th Street. It was built around the turn of the century, large oak-framed windows, two sun porches. The day I carried my bags through the door, my landlord was painting the kitchen, white paint on his fingers, his hair. I loved the place immediately. But for the carpets. I picked up the corner of the living room carpet and found beautiful hardwood floors underneath.

I asked him if he would take up the carpets. He was reluctant, but agreed, and we set about lifting the carpets the next day, pulling out carpet tacks, and scraping off dried glue. I was thrilled: the floors — the original hundred-year-old floors — were in wonderful shape. My landlord began to talk about bringing in a sander and then spreading a verathane finish. No no, I insisted, none of that. These are just fine. I like the scratches, the spots just as they are. I want the history of the families who have lived here, to keep walking through this home.

On his way out, we stood talking on the frontporch. At some point, I looked above my head. On the doorframe was a *mezzuzeh*. My eyes filled with tears. I was pleased, surprised. Jews had lived here before me.

What's that? he asked. It contains Jewish blessings, I said, they're rolled up inside. Anyone who enters here, is blessed.

I've owned this place fifteen years, he said, never noticed it.

After he left, I removed the layers of paint from the old mezzuzeh, and I tacked up mine, just a little below, and parallel to it.

Let me tell you another story. My landlord's heritage is German. I am Jewish. He is a kind, thoughtful, hard-working man. I am a kind, thoughtful, hard-working woman. We are friends. He came over last week to fix my oven. (This is not a metaphor. This really happened.) One of the heating elements had exploded one day, and needed replacing. I'd been working at the kitchen table, before he arrived, writing, thinking, reading about the Holocaust. We talked, as he leaned in and out of his toolbox and the oven.

When I was in the Army, he said, I visited Auschwitz. It scared me.

In what way, I asked.

Well, you know that I'm of German descent, he said. And I'm the kind of guy who likes to do things right. It scared me to think of what I might have done, had I lived there then, and been indoctrinated into those values. It scared me.

He fitted the new heating element into the bottom of the oven, and latching up his toolbox, he said, I have a friend here in La Crosse who doesn't believe it happened.

What didn't, I asked.

The Holocaust. At least not to the extent they claim.

Are you kidding? (I had heard and read that there were people who thought this way.) What about all the documentation, the photographs?

Well, *he* would say, you can always take a picture of the same 400 bodies over and over.

❧

This is the shape of the Fear That Doesn't Go Away: I thought about moving out. Packing my books, *You're only allowed one bag*, leaving in the night, that night.

Let me tell you another story. My grandmother left in the night. She was 13. It was just before the turn of the century, in Russia. Carpenters were building the floor of the house I was living in in Wisconsin, when my grandmother Bessie Weisman left Seredna, a little town on the Russian Polish border. She had lived there with her parents, her sisters, brothers, they were Orthodox Jews, they owned a small general store, they sold thread, barley, coffee. It was a time of pogroms. One day, she was helping her father in the store, and some Russian soldiers came in, ordered some coffee. She carried it to them from the Samovar, and one of them grabbed her breast. She spilled (threw?) the hot coffee at him, burned his face, he threw her to the floor, and beat her. It was after that that she asked her family why they stayed there. She wanted to leave, this was not new, she had had enough of pogroms. They said no, this was their home, they had been there for generations, they would stay. She wrote her uncle in New York, asked him for boatfare, she would come to New York, and work until she paid back his money. She walked 30 miles to the nearest port, got on a boat, by herself, and came to Ellis Island. She was 13 years old.

A month later, her sisters left too. They went to Poland. To a town called Lodz. 400,000 Jews were murdered by the Nazis at Chelmo, a town 50 miles NW of Lodz. Two Jews survived. They were not my aunts.

The rest of the family who stayed in Seredna were taken to Auschwitz. *You're only allowed one bag*, leaving in the night, that night.

1996

HOME, WHAT IT COSTS

I'm not good at closing doors, you once wrote me, *and when I see you,*
it's not so much the memories of our life together that surface,
but rather the feeling that we've strayed so very far from home.

for Federico

The drive to camp in the desert alone is not without fear, the dirt roads
can wash out, I've been warned, and the forecast is for rain, but the car is
packed, and my obsession has teeth. The road into the canyon is red rock
chips and clay. I go slow, at first, against the brutal bumps, then take my
foot off the brake, hold the wheel hard, ignore the car's rattle, and go
ahead, go straight ahead. I am heading home. I have forgotten
where home is.

Years ago, I left our life on First Avenue, left you tending tomatoes
in the back garden, rooted to a life that no longer included my growth.
You wanted marriage, my undivided energy. What I wanted was you
and a home and to write poetry, to teach, to earn enough to support
myself. It was likely I'd have to move. Perhaps it is easier to leave
someone you no longer love.

I have come alone to this canyon, a grieving woman, to visit the homes
of those who lived here a thousand years ago. I'm not sure why. I have
learned to listen to the risings under my skin, the pull. The ancient ones
who lived here built their homes out of sandstone rock and pine trees,
and for those trees, had to walk more than fifty miles. They would cut
one down, leave it to dry on the mesa, one year later, return, carry it home.

It is six in the morning. Here in clay soil, I build a fire, boil tea, the sun
gains weight in the sky. I climb the ruins, the ancient ones teach me:
in their kiva, they germinate seedlings of corn. How perfect, to seed
corn in a sacred room. I learn I must plant the seedlings of my new life
in a round sacred place. How does this fit? When I think of home,
I still think of you.

The night sky fills with stars, each distinct, separate. No moon.
I wake in the night, the full moon has risen. It has liquified the stars,
they stretch the sky in waves. I rise, walk bare across the red rock.
I dream you are a tree. I am carrying the loss of you home.

Chaco Canyon, New Mexico, 1995

Sam, Returns

I am sitting in the kitchen, eating rhubarb apple
pie, and a man's hand comes up behind me, covers
my eyes, it's my father's hand, I know it immediately,
smelling of shaving cream and topsoil, his fingers thick
warm, I turn, holding his hand, I've not seen him in years,
his face round, shy even, *I've got something for you*, he says,
he's come back from the dead, *a surprise*, he says, *I didn't have
it ready when I left eleven years ago*, and it's a play, my

father has written a play for me, it's the story of his life, and
it's being performed in my living room, four actors, they
are sitting cross-legged on the carpet, and one of them,
a young girl, her back to me, gets up, turns around and it's
Ali, my sweet Ali, in light white jeans, she is twelve years
old, she runs over to us, throws her arms around her grandfather
and me, and skips back to her place in the play, my

father is leaving, I want him to stay, he is leaving, and with him,
the play

"Jews are gypsies, they wander," my neighbor, sitting beside me at the library last night, says. This is the same neighbor, last year, I'm backing out of my parking space at the market, I'm on my way to the frame store. I have a sepia photo of my father's father, the tailor Ben Plonsky, with his twelve brothers and sisters. I stop the car, say hello. He says, "What's that?" The photo is on the seat beside me. "I'm on my way to have it framed," I say. I pick it up, hold it out the window so he can see it. "My grandfather, his brothers, his sisters." We look at it together. They are dressed up in high-necked suits and dresses for the photo, posing for the camera in three rows, standing and sitting. "My father, there," I point, "the kid sitting on the floor." He leans down, looks closer. "They are SOBs," he says. "SOBs?" "Yes," he says. "Straight Off The Boat." I look at him. He is serious. "Yes, I know," I say. "Isn't it wonderful!" Last night at the library, he asks, "Am I going to be in your book?"

Outside my Wisconsin kitchen window the sun is ice blue, I am rinsing
beans for soup. An ad on the back cover of a magazine asks, *where in
the world is the information superhighway taking us?* So I sit down
at my laptop, plug into the world wide web, with a name like that
you'd think I'd get a gorgeous spidery web holding the earth, but no,
I get a home address that reads *http colon slash slash www dot,*
a home address that isn't home, that forgot it is language

So I hear my daughter's voice, saying *get over it, mom,* and I do, I read
the address, *http colon slash slash www dot.* I sight-read it, for it
doesn't slip luxuriously into my brain and come out making sense, as in
senses, as in running my eyes over some welcome mat made of hemp,
as in touching hand-painted clay tiles next to the door lamp. I step over
the letters, the home address, the box of words leeched of its lushness,
tools sitting on the doorstep. I enter this home this highway of homes

Later, I am walking the river bank, the Mississippi. Overhead, an
eagle, O winged sister. It is a surprise to me how much I love winter.
The hush when the snow is down, the snap of my boots across a field
of rooted oak, air mapping the inside of my lungs. It is dusk. I left soup
beans soaking on the stove. Downriver, I see lights inside homes along
the waterway clicking on

1996

INVENTION

for Molly and Mike

I wish you love, the bright kind, the filled with light kind, the
beside you in the night kind, the side-splitting laughter upside-
down ferris wheel ride kind, and the wide kind, the expandable
elasticized durable tough as hide, work out the rough times kind

I wish you words, the dear kind, the have no fear kind, the I'll
always love you kind, the clear kind, the I hear you kind, the
we're different and don't always have to agree, supporting
each other to grow kind

I wish you health, the working up a sweat running to the
breadstore kind, the organic food kind, the tall tree clean air
kind, the ball's in the air, gimme a break, tearing
down the stress, music is a must kind

I wish you kids, the wealthy in health kind, the such a
cute toosh kind, the gritty hands from sands at the beach,
singing at the table, arms around your neck, strong
as a trans-Atlantic cable kind

the Sunday morning lolling in bed kind, the redhot chili
bumping car willies, all day long sillies, dollies and bikes,
lollies and Nikes, and years and years and years of the
I remember when I was a kid kind

I wish you vision, the let's re-create marriage kind, the let's re-
imagine the institution from scratch kind, the loosed from its
moorings, no more obscuring handed-down versions kind,
the turn of the twenty-first century, you've got all you need
to invent the exponentury Molly and Mike kind

1994

QUIETLY

for Barbara and Terry

And it happened quietly when it happened, this love
of yours, your eyes on each other, quiet and inward
as a path home, and it was, and it is, here today, this home
you begin here together, in this synagogue set in a garden,
blessed under the trees, under the sky, under the sun,
standing you two beside each other, two two and not two
but two families becoming one, creating the fruit of the vine,
two loving friends, at the center of the circle of your friends,
we who love you we who have been blessed with all you
have given us these so many years, our lives made peace
with you in it, we who come here today to bless you
on your path home to each other, and to us, and
the sound of the bride and the sound of the groom,
the jubilant sound of lovers joined under the chupah

1998

III

Turning

> ... (T)he circumstances of North America ... in a decade
> that began with the Gulf War and that has witnessed accelerated social
> disintegration, the lived effects of an economic system out of control and anti
> human at its core ... Material profit finally has no use for other values, in fact
> reaps profit from social incoherence and atomization, and from erosion
> of human bonds of trust − in language or anything else ...
>
> — Adrienne Rich

I Can

I can move the feet I carry with me I can move the hands
the luggage in the closet the bed under the window the car
in the driveway the nose that sits on my face I can move
the laptop that sits on my table the flowers that open to me
each morning I open the door and say how are you this
morning beautiful flower how did I get to be so lucky as to
have you in my life I can move the book beside me the
book beside me but what of the newspapers growing heavy
heavier on the doorstep, I can no longer move them, lift
them, I cannot move the dirty work going on in Congress,
I cannot move the chopping blocks, the school lunch trays,
the orphanage doors, orphans? I always thought orphans
had no mothers no fathers where did they stash the bodies,
I cannot move the bodies the bodies are everywhere,
cut cut poor women their children from welfare, cut cut
farmworkers, their children from school from medical care,
cut cut affirmative action, cut the small gains we've made,
I cannot stop the knives of Congress working overtime,
overtime, the slick slicing of the NEA, the NEH,
the clank of deregulating, privatizing, downsizing,
speeding up, forcing overtime, the lean the mean,
the laying off the workers, the elders, they will not stop,
I cannot stop I cannot move the thundercloud of skin
the branch lowering its head bucking for profit —
legislators, just who do you think you are —
you cannot I cannot I can I can we can we can we will
move your greed it bleeds a hemorrhage

1995

47

THE HEARING

*Welfare reform was invented in Wisconsin. I was there. I read this poem
as protest testimony before Wisconsin Senate hearings on the "Wisconsin Works"
welfare reform bill, 1995. The legislation passed, became the blueprint
for California in 1997, and across the U.S.*

we're here to talk about poor women and work, poor
women and work, as if they don't work, but that's
another story, we're here to talk about poor women,
so let's talk, shall we? not in the polite mid-western way,
the smile on our face, how nice we are to find work for
women, the dignity of work for women, how American
we are to find work for women, a way out of welfare, how
nice we are, let's talk, shall we? what's the plan here, work
for women, what work? young people with three college
degrees are out of work, people in their fifties with thirty
years experience are out of work, what jobs, what work is
there for women with no skills, outside of mothering that
is, and we'll make sure it stays that way, we'll cut them off
from college, and we'll build in a little provision here, all
welfare moms who can't find a job, well we'll just find
them a job, won't we, we'll get into bed with industry,
and provide a slave labor force, did I say that? did I say,
a drone class, a drudge class, dignity, what dignity, let's talk,
shall we? and once these women, these poor women get
a job, and the working conditions get worse, as they will,
and if these women dare speak out, well, industry will just
fire them, won't they, and then we'll build in another little
provision here, case workers will, and I quote, remove
children from the home if they're not adequately
financially supported, remove them from the home,
and aren't we nice, we'll build orphanages for these
children, and the women, the women, the poor women,
they'll be out on the streets, dignity? do I hear dignity?
do I hear work? work? let's talk straight here:

I believe you're selling an illusion, it's been done before, it's been done to my people, brought to a concentration camp, the words above the door, *arbeit macht frei, work makes you free*, it's been done before

in our country, in this state, we do it differently, we do it politely, we smile and say aren't we nice Americans?

1995

The great hall fills with people come to see the show. We sit,
silent, each in our seats, eyes to the front. The empty stage
empties our faces. I turn in my seat, look behind me: rows
of faces, and above me, rows of faces, the balcony. It is leaking.
I say to the man beside me, *Look the balcony is leaking.*
He doesn't hear me. He's watching the empty stage.
The balcony bulges. It is leaking lava, a narrow stream,
steaming down into the crowd. They don't seem to feel it,
continue to watch the stage. I turn to the man beside me,
Let's get out of here, I say. He doesn't hear me. I begin to
think he is dead. I poke him in the stomach. *Come on,* I say,
I'm getting out of here. He doesn't move. I pull him by his belt
toward me. *Yes,* he says, and we gather the suitcases, run down
the aisle, out the door, and grab a bus.

1995

TURNING

the smell of something dead
is entering our house

something large and loose
and carrying a pole, hung
with damp skins, unable to dry out

it is shriveling us now, this
dark thing we have carried
unknowingly into our home

I have known it and not known it
couldn't see its face

the smell of something dead
is entering our house,
and shadows, the late afternoon kind,
nod across the garden grasses

Rainwater, Re-Collecting

For weeks the heat has been endless as toads
and suddenly, at one in the morning, the window
is ticking with rain. In my nightgown and bare feet
I carry pots out to the back porch, down the stairs.
The backyard hangs its budding flowers loose as first teeth
and I am squatting in grass with pots gathering rain,
watching the moonrise. In the morning, I climb the shelves
for an old decanter, pour in rainwater drop by drop. My head
is filled with running mountain pines, streams, and wind.
A sip, and my tongue is coated with dead spoons, gasoline.

THE BLACK SUN AND GLOBAL WARMING, ONE THEORY

so here it is, she said, walking down pueblo del sur in taos, new mexico, here it is, she said, and squatted on the sidewalk in front of the gem store, and there it was, a black sun, face-up on the concrete, its rays rubbing her feet, asking to be picked up, which she did, looping its great circumference round her waist, and off she went down the street, the crowds following her, asking, well, what do we do with a black sun? do, she said? we love it, lean into it, ask it why it's here, why taos, why now, why late on a summer afternoon in nineteen-ninety-five

so she took it home and loved it, shined its circle with organic waxes, combed its rays a hundred strokes a day, in the old ways, and talked to it of her friends, henry and tina, artelia and robin, and julian, carol, and marti'n, and it nodded and dimmed and dozed off and on, so she fed it bits of blue corn and news of overheated turkeys exploding in wisconsin and it began to shimmy in her hands, and the radio lit up with broadcasts of elders dying of the heat at their tv sets in chicago, and the black sun whirled and buzzed

and friends began to drop by with sitings of other black suns landing in the rio grande gorge, and it came to her what she must do, so she carried it outside in the night and strapped it to the roof of her car, and the two of them blazed their way along hiway 68 and 84 to 96 and 44 then 57 in to chaco canyon, chaco canyon, the sun told her, and, with her left arm out the window, she fed it more kernels of blue corn, and it told her thousand-year-old tales of the ancient ones, the sun watchers, and fajada butte, their golden sandstone sun station

and the black sun gyrated on the rooftop, and reminisced about lodging at the butte, its words, *dead friends*, trailing off along the rocks in the road, and suddenly it began to smoke and talk politics into the night, its great sighs, winds howling in the desert night air, filling the canyon and her ears and waking up folks who listened at their windows for miles around, soon, it said, soon it will be discovered that murdered bodies give off heat, that the cries of the dead ones, through the centuries, have been rising, scorching the sun

and it revved her engine and the radio, moving the dial to news now coming in from
washington, dc, of politicians, stripping naked from the heat, building cages, clanking
and rattling, working overtime to enforce poverty

and that did it, that did it, that set the sun off, it burst its bindings, picked up desert
winds, blew itself flew itself off ahead of her, and when she pulled up at the base
of fajada butte, black suns were everywhere, coming in from bosnia, beirut, south
africa, new york, los angeles, la crosse, and she said, here it is

black suns, setting up camp on the peak of the sunstone, pressed themselves — a circle
of suns — into the rock, and when they'd burned it white heat hot, they beamed it
at the eighty-seven people who run the world, and soldered compassion into
the valves of their hearts

Chaco Canyon, 1995

DOWN THE ROAD, THE VOICES

after seeing the play, *Down The Road*,
by Lee Blessing, San Diego, CA.

down the road, the play. two cane chairs. a motel room, two journalists. he makes a move on her. it's not professional, she says, wraps her legs around him. you interview him first, she says. interview who? he's killed 19 women, at least. oh. and what did you use to kill her. a knife, i stabbed her seven times, how dare he, from behind, in the car, i asked to come out to the car, told her i was a magazine photographer, i planned it, put my bag in the back seat floor, wedged it in. i asked her to move the front seat forward

she had to sit down in it, how dare he, who does he think he is, this is just a play, my cheeks are wet, i have to take off my shoes, my hands are sweating. how did you kill her. i took her head off with a nylon cord. where. in the kitchen. there's a sink there. i know how not to make a mess. i am here alone. nineteen. at least. my hands. it is dark here. the women here, we do not look at each other. why did you stop dumping them there at silver lake. i went back. why did you go back. i forgot

something. an anklet, i wanted it. the bodies were in different states of, decomposition? yes. they had been dragged there, by, uh, animals, different kind of hunters, i was the first hunter. it's too tight, i have to take off my watch. my arms are dead. i am here alone. i can't look at anyone. why a ten year old, why not. it could've been anyone, it didn't matter,

i needed someone. she was there. why didn't you just rape them. it wouldn't have been enough. my legs are dead. what it is like driving the freeway at two a.m. i own the road, driving into that widening

moment of possibility, i am here alone, she is mine, i own her, i can do what i want with her, i get out of the car, the night is mine, she is mine, her purse is mine, the contents of her purse is mine, I determine her breath, and when I'm tired of her breath, i take it, i take it, i'm taking this, i'm sitting here and taking this, we're going to use him, remember, we're going to write about this, use him, she says, and they'll remember me, a hundred years from now, you'll be dead, and they'll remember me, they eat it up. the papers, they'll make a

movie, a tv movie that's the best, they'll remember me, they'll come, they'll eat it up, the women have silver hair. i can't breathe. you killed her, threw her out the car door. i broke all the rules. i can't sit still. stop talking about it, stop, i will tell him to stop, to shut up, i won't listen. this is a play, I tell myself, be still, it breaks the mood for the actors. i won't write about it. we are his charge. he kills for the charge. i kill women. not any more. we write about him, they buy it, they all buy it, they eat it up. i won't write about it, i won't be still, why is my heart pounding. my hands are dead. sweating. they used to sweat like that in high school before a date, what if

i have nothing to say. and you're all alone, no one can help you, they put the hood over your head though you tell them not to, your sweat smells different than it ever did before,

they put cotton up your ass, a rubber band around your penis, so that what's inside you will stay inside you. my feet i can't feel my feet. i tied her, from behind, her hands, her feet, i taped her mouth. say no, the next time he opens his mouth i'm going to say no, shut up, i'm leaving i won't write this, yes, tear up the tapes, pull the ribbon, tear them up, tear his words, tear his pride in them, his lousy, yes, burn them, burn him

did i say him, i meant them, the words. no i meant him, burn him, he can't do this, they can't do this, and we sit here on and on, silent in the dark, we are here alone and not alone, the silent women and the arm-crossed men, and the play is over, they're clapping. my hands won't work. i don't want to clap. what are they clapping for. i have to clap, they did a great job. i don't want to clap. i'm supposed to clap, it's what we do in a theater after a play, clap, ok i'll clap, my hands don't work, my feet don't work,

where are my shoes, they're all walking out, i'm crying again, thank god i'm crying again, i cried the first time he told how he killed her, i cried, he was killing me, he was every man who'd ever killed any woman and i was every woman who'd ever been killed by a man, and i cried and after that, i didn't cry, after that parts of my body got deader and deadened and i'm crying again thank god i'm crying, are you alright? i'm not alright, we're not alright, i don't want to be alright, cry for all the years i never cried, for all the years i was cut up in the smallest ways, the words that got me from behind, they knew how not to make a mess, is she ok? no i'm

not ok, i'm a body here in the mud decomposing and i can still cry, my legs are shaking, my shoes, i can fit in my shoes, zip them up, walk, what a play, thank you yes, no, i'm not angry at the writer, i'm a writer too, thank, tell him, tell the actors, they ask a lot of an audience, to sit still, to feel badly about sitting still, i'll not sit still, i'll not sit in my seat, be silent in the dark theater of the classroom, i'll not teach writing as writing but as mud, what does it feel like, how is it under there, speak, write, don't be silent, write it down, i'm not alone, we're not alone, he will shut up when we shut him up

she couldn't
stand it anymore
this writhing
this writing
words coming out of her fingers
droppings on the page
shit, it stank
and she knew
it was useless
what could words do
with all this going on
and what was this anyway
writing it all down
a woman in the desert
watering sand

BELLY OPEN BELLY

for Jacob,
four months old

How far away is
the world, you
could be asking,
the nightlight
beside your bed,
your eyes wide
as your belly is open
this evening as I change
you, my nose rubbing your
belly, the old game, the nose,
your rounded pear belly,
and your laughter loosening
the walls of the world,
how far away is the
warborn world
from this newborn
well of trust

1999

IV

POSSIBILITY

The energy crackled, the same kind of energy needed to shift continental plates . . .

— Joy Harjo

POSSIBILITY

In 1991, Fort Ord, a military base in California for 80 years, is closed down.
In 1994, California State University Monterey Bay opens on its grounds.

Who would have thought it possible, to call the troops together
in the mess hall one morning, Monterey fog not yet burned off,
and say *we're closing down the base*

Who would have thought it possible to load guns and missiles
into crates, artillery onto trucks, cannons onto flatbed railroad cars
to board up the windows of the barracks

      And the grass grew long and quickly took over the fields,
      thousands of soldiers marching down Inter-Garrison road
      dwindled down to twelve then none

Who would have thought it possible to transform the chapel
that held the Panama coffin of Sargeant William Delaney Gibbs
      into a music hall that swells with the sound of the poetry
      of Sekou Sundiata and the sax of John Purcell

Who would have thought it possible to turn a
blood bank *when we go to war we carry with us our own blood*

into an environmental research lab. And students,
      after the microscopes and studies, marching
      against strawberry blood laced with methyl bromide

Who would have thought it possible to board up the soldiers'
club with its great oakwood bar and glass walls leaning the ocean
at Fort Ord, named after a general "famed as an Indian fighter"

And, two years later, for Andrea Woody, a student
      in the Institute of Community Memory, to dig down, to research,
      to call her Cascade grandmother back to her, to hold her
      photograph, her letters in her hands

Who would have thought it possible
to transform jeep and tank garages into public art studios
the radio transmitter station into state of the art computer tech
the artillery vault into an on-line library
the battalion headquarters into the president's office

Who would have thought it possible
to transform a survival training station into a child care center
　　　to turn parachutes into small sweaters hanging from hooks,
　　　　gas masks into little laughing shoving mouths at the water faucet

Who would have thought, in the unused rooms of the campus,
soldiers' beds would be piled, years and years of soldiers' beds,
mattresses still ticking with cigarette burns

Who would have thought
students would now walk back and forth with their books
past these boarded windows, and inside, the eyelids
of the war dead would open, flutter like hummingbirds

1997

COMPUTER DANCERS

CSUMB Vision Statement: "CSU Monterey Bay is committed to diversity, particularly working class, low income, and historically underserved students." Thirty percent of our students are Latina/o, Chicano/a, from Salinas, Castroville, Watsonville, California.

Moving, tipping into the twenty-first century, way out here on the west coast, tipping into the Pacific. My students are wise to me, a low-tech writer in a high tech university, they the brilliant computer dancers on the web, the lovely fluidity of DELETE and CUT and PASTE, dear dear students, emerging writers, coming up in California, in earthquake territory, they bring up and out their life stories long erased, the daughters the sons of farmworkers, the days the years working the fields, the lost knees, backs, the whirr of helicopters, pesticides fulminating their lungs their lives, and they will tele-conference with me, across the state, the country, we will, all of us, emerge, erupt, who knows where, on the other side of the millennium, go in good health, as my mother used to say, we're building. And we're doing it together, SAVE.

1997

"In the first years of the twenty-first century, it was discovered
that voices, all the unheard ones, didn't die at the end of life.
Instead, they spent thousands of years, wandering underground.
. . . It was an earthquake like no other."

— Frances Payne Adler, from "Raising The Tents," 1993

for Julie Bliss, in search of Mary Garner Cole, 1863 – 1939

You are a search party traveling back for your great
grandmother, for years you've been studying Choctaw,
you hear faint directions cracking open, you track them back,
uncover them in ditches of history books, the songs the whispers
of family stories, a name, a date, a town inscribed in a bible,
a page in a diary, homestead documents in a thin drawer,
calling you under the canyons the coasts of California to
Iowa to Missouri, and in your face the clocks are clanging
the docks banging together, wind, waves, and fluid fields
of corn hang over hang under you, you pitch the tents of your
questions. *Grandmother, speak to me,* you say, and you can hear
her, calling you back for the voices, for the years she's been
chanting Choctaw, not stripped from your family, not lost
to the conquerors, not lost to marriage nor to gods, she's calling
you, your great grandmother, knowing you've retrieved the eyes
to see her, the ears to hear her, her words, to have them surface
the centuries, the years between you, you will crack the dry earth
of silence, tell the stories she hands you, broken stories no longer,
no longer leeched of her truth, her blood no longer sapped from you

1998

ALL MY RELATIONS

for my colleagues, returning from vacation

and the night before returning, how was your heart
as you leaned over the sink, washed your face, or later,
turned down the lamp, did some sense of dread rise
in you, remembering the electronic mailbox weighted
with messages and more coming in even as you
answer, the nights leaving your desk long after dark,
the clank of the door and you look up, surprised by the moon,
not that it's that late but that it isn't on a screen,
doing twelve things at once, and the bite in your gut
of no sense of completion, that round thing,
remembering the student's face darkening when you
turn her away, run to committee meetings, the ache
in your chest to put students first, isn't that why we're here,
the yearning for just plain time to think,
remembering waking at night your head tangled
with meetings, phone calls to make, who said what, what
you said, what you'll say, and you get up, find a pen, unload
these lists and still you can't sleep,
remembering your neck in a knot sitting too long
at the computer, salads day after day eaten at your desk,
working through lunch, through dinner, remembering
some wonderful thing someone said at a meeting, wanting
to know them better, each of you saying so, and it doesn't happen,
the ache to have a life

and me? i think of my grandmother bessie sitting on a low chair
with her legs apart her elbows out her hands on her thighs
her stockings rolled down below her knees *I vorked tvelf
sometimes sewenteen hours a day in de shop sorting buttons*,
she would say in thick yiddish-english, switching her v's and her w's,
vot a life, and she would nod her head, shake her finger and say,
but you, you francela, you vill go to college, you vill not do such a ting,
and here I am doing such a thing

I know you came here with a dream in your hand
I too came with a dream   it had a round shape
it walked with a spring in its step, it laughed easily
all my relations would be here   and you are
you are the place I dreamed, the workplace love of my life

I cry for the tangle we are making.
bessie would say, *don't tell dem I told you*
but dey're giwin it to you, too few vorkers on de line

1997

Slow

In the last years of the twentieth century, the pleasure of slowness
disappeared, sucked out of people's lives like fresh air. Oxygen bars
began to be popular, but no matter how large a cannister was ordered,
the metronome had been advanced. One young woman was overheard
impatient with baths *I keep waiting for something to happen,* she said

Windshield wipers and computer cursors were set on high, seats
in coffee shops removed. People stood at tall counters, tipped back
their one ounce shot of coffee, were out the door. Newspaper and book
sales plummeted. Who had the time? A young man on a street corner,
reported to be murmuring *I am a wind-up doll with a key in my back*

1998

"The word that best describes all of you is 'exhausted.'
What are the new silences?"

— Tillie Olsen, at the Modern Languages Association
(MLA) conference, Dec. 1994, on the 20th anniversary
of the publication of her book *Silences,* 1974.

Our lives are snowing for miles on the highways,
the computer is blowing its horn, baby, and paper towers
around the world are yawning across the screen, erasing
the childhood stories we have known, the bank is roasting
our wallets red, workers don't scream, our mouths are filled
with discs, spigots have been pushed into our chests, metal cans
hung from them, our wages drip dripping are being drained

1998

WHAT'S A MOTHER TO DO

Written and performed in response to the university's plan
for computerized distance learning, that still needed to place
our students at the center of its design.

What's a mother to do but love you, hug you round the waist,
sit you down and tell you a story or two about a lot of us
folks who never did go and sit on these learning steps
with all the books you teach, and the fine way you come up
out of one of these places, with lit-up eyes and a way of talking
that makes folks in the work world sit up and listen

Well now, wouldn't you know, bless her, my young one
has gone and finished high school, and it's her time to go out
into that worker world, and she's carrying me with her, right
there on her shoulders, and I'm sitting up there and cheering

Now, we know you have these fancy computer screens
and we're pleased you're teaching our kids to move that kind
of knowing around in that kind of world, and that they're learning
all about where their family comes from, and why and how they're
here, calling up the stories, we're mighty happy you're doing that,
and that you're also teaching them about a lot of fine folks
around the world, and how we're all gonna get by together,
and keep the world clean and fair-minded, and honey,

what's a mother to do, I ask you. I know it seems to you to make
a whole lot of sense to use those screens to speak knowing
into my baby's sweet head, but now that we're kin of yours, y'hear,
we need to talk around awhile about how this is going to,
like the main man said, *break the mold of learning,* about how
long-distance screens are going to fold and mold our kids

Listen, they're used to in-the-flesh learning. You need to know
who we are and who our folks are and where we've all been to
and done and said, and I say, any big change you make, you
need to keep talking to us and to our young ones, to make
sure they get what they need to go out there and shine

Guess you hear me saying I want a warm body next to my child,
teaching her, same as everyone else that's come up through
the highest schooling, not some screen beeping in her eyes,
this world is still about warm bodies, I tell you, and no kid of mine
is going to sit in a room with solely a screen for a teacher

What's a mother to do but love you, hug you round the waist
and say, honey, that's not why I sent my child here, not at all,
I didn't send her here to have you push her sweet butt faster
through the door, y'know, in and out car wash?

And here, listen, is the gnawing in my heart: just when our kinfolk
are coming up for learning, why do you want to give them less
teachers, and push them through faster, why, answer me that

1998

Enter

In the cool leaf of quiet they enter us,
in the plumed air of trust they enter us,
those who have lived here on this coastland
before us, those who have passed, walking
to us up the stairs of the past, up the layers
of the earth, one culture and then another,
name them — Ohlone, Esselen, Salinan,
Costanoan, Mexican, Spanish, U.S. army –
their ears their eyes clotted with moss, the clank
the clatter of voices rising, they carry up to us
the birds the drizzled corn of their children

And they who have been here before us, sitting
now as they are with us, seeping with algae
and the past, they hand over to us their children
and their children's children, their tears, the tunnels
of their laughter, the coughing, the fevers, the fires,
the songs, *we are here, know you know us*

In the cool leaf of quiet they enter us,
in the plumed air of trust they enter us
Be firm in what brought you here,
we brought you here

1998

SHELF OF THE MILLENNIUM

for Cece and Tony

I walk the long spit of beach in Big Lagoon, sand and not sand,
the beach is pebbles that pull my shoes under, each step a moist
connect with the sea. It's early morning, the sky not yet full-open
to sun, fog sits on the shore rocks. I am inside this, it is inside me.
The ocean to my left, waves open like large mouths, they crest,
they roar. The lagoon to my right, I lean against the upturned
root of a Sitka spruce, lagoon water laps the shore like breaths,
in and out, in again and out. This is Yurok land, they who
called this place *Oketo* meaning *where it is calm.*

Today is the second to last day of the year, it is slipping itself
under the shelf of the millennium, and it comes to me like a mirror,
how many years ago, fifteen, I was locked in a stagnant
lagoon life, a pseudo-safe life, and an ocean roared inside me.
Today I recognize I have flipped the waters — the lagoon is now
inside me, this time clear and calm, and the ocean roars outside.

And the roar these past months at our university, and those trying
to tilt the foundation we're building, no you will not chip away
at what we've fused together these last five years, no you will not
pull us under. And what we have sown here, our students tall
as spruce carry so much with them, wish I could find the words,
what words, words, willow willow words words, words slim
and sitka strong, students carry with them like fold-up chairs
from one room to another, from one world to another, they
carry this this lens this this chest of questions, this what
do I need to know in relation to you, your history, your
culture, what you value, what you believe, my history,
my culture, what I value, what I believe, and a way of
listening to each other, a way of holding words between us
like a spit of beach, our lives water roaring on one side,
calm on the other, finding the balance between us,
the kiss-connect beneath our feet.

No you will not chip away at what we have fused together,
and it comes back to me, a mirror, I am in the Metro ,
the Gare du Nord Metro in Paris, I have just gotten off
the Metro, it is five o'clock rush hour, hundreds of people
around me rushing by, and I look down, my purse is open,
the zipper unzipped, my wallet is gone, gone, *completement
disparu,* a sweat climbs like fingers up my back, I look around
me, behind me, a woman, a blue checkered scarf around her head,
she says nothing, she points to a man in front of us, he is tall, thin,
wearing a black three-piece suit, his suit jacket around his shoulders,
his arms are swinging free, he is hurtling away from us, I look back
at the woman, she says nothing, shakes her head, as if to say, yes,
yes, I saw him, this is the man who stole your wallet, I look back
at the man, tall, thin, slipping away into the crowd hurrying toward home.

And from somewhere inside me, a voice, I had gone that morning
to the fishmarket, heard the shrill cry of the woman who sold cod
and crab and carried home this voice, *Donnez le moi,* I yell to him
in my jagged French, this man in the crowd, his back to me,
Give it to me, I say, teeth in my voice, I roar at him again,
his back is to me, he is rushing away from me, *Donnez le moi,*
and he turns, this man who could not know I was talking to him,
he turns, he stops, he puts his hand in his suit jacket pocket, and I
shiver, what have I done, I ask myself, omygod, he has a gun,
he's going to shoot me, what have I done, and a sweat rises,
and he walks toward me, his hand outstretched, what have I done,
and he hands me my wallet, says nothing, turns and hurries himself
into the crowd, disappears. And here it is, my wallet, he hasn't had
time to take anything from it, all my money is here, the crowd closes
around me, they are congratulating me in French, arms around my
shoulders, the man is gone, and in the bustle of a Metro station,
I am stunned with the voice that has risen from me, safe as steel.

I am no longer stunned, these years later. I am my voice.
I am these calm waters, breathing in and out, in again and out.
The ocean roars sometimes outside me and I walk this spit of land.
Despite those who would tilt us, we will continue to carry
our folding chairs, breathe calm water, breathe Sitka spruce.

They tell me the Yurok called this place *Oketo,*
where it is calm. They also called this place *O-pyuweg,*
meaning *where they dance.* Where they dance, where we dance.
And the day slips under the shelf of the year. Tomorrow is the last
day of the millennium, I am here in Big Lagoon with my friends,
in a cabin on the cusp of time, a cabin in the north California
coastlands, wet with promise, wet with lush friendship,
our lives roaring and calm. Tomorrow night we'll build
a fire on the beach with sea-washed and dried wood,
we'll welcome the new millennium together, and we'll dance.

Big Lagoon, Arcata, California
Dec. 30, 1999

V

WINTER GROUND

For peace is something we already have,
like a summer bulb buried deep in winter ground.

— Kim Zorn Caputo

NEW YEAR

Big Sur

I've come to the canyon of muscled sycamore,
come without words to the weeks of waning summer,
come to surrender my deepest silence

At four in the morning, I climb from sleep
to a hill high above the rocking flesh of ocean.
What float the nightboat. What full entry the moon.

Out of my mouth, the squeak of baby swallows

RAW

Three days ago,
Wednesday night, eight
thirty, and the doctor in my ear, *it is cancer,*
she says, I hear the words, I don't hear, my pen
writes *cancer* as she speaks, this is not
happening, *small, just six millimeters,*
sweat my hands sweat,
alert as microphones
underwater

2000

What Is It

What is it when what
you fear most in the world
happens, when cancer comes –

Sorrow
like spores of razor-wings
in my lungs, my eyes

2000

A Visitation

Six days after learning
I have breast cancer,
I wake to the night's sounds

the river rushing over rocks

a single bird (a hermit thrush?)
in the maple tree outside my window

its song six discrete sounds and a refrain
and I hear (from where?) its translation –
I promise you will live, you will live

and the river and the song and the sun
coming up slow as patience

and words these last few days
finally come through the casing, the tube
of breast cancer I'd been slipping into,
fear eroding me from much of who I am

I will not erode

and the river,
insistent, constant, coursing

Mackenzie River, Oregon, 2000

Firm Ease

I stand beside the Mackenzie River rapids, watch it rush over rocks,
watch three women in a fishing boat: one, in the middle, rowing; one
sitting in the prow, watching for danger; one standing, fishing, throwing
out her line; and the rower, her hands on the oars with firm ease, she
steers the boat sideways, not head on, into the rapids

2000

I am a woman who is pathetic, a doll made of dish rags, a heap
of tears on the stairs, in the washroom leaning over the sink,
I am a woman who stops on the packed-mud ocean path,
who stands beside the wild blue heron perched on a pile of sand,
both of us still, staring out to sea. I am a woman who grieves
for my lost energy, sorrow seeping out of me, grumbling
water weeping my walls, I am a woman who cuts back
the fuchsia hanging in pots, even the fuchsia stems weep

2001

De-Briefing

Her breasts
swallowed the cancer
and she was sent to spy
across the border of death.

The night of her return, she
could not remember what
she had seen there,
a forgetting only in the narration.
Her breasts had turned to glass,
been shot at, shattered.
Her fingers had turned to twigs.
She snapped them off
and dropped them.
Her stomach, she said,
was tin corrugated washboard.
The electrical wiring of her heart
had re-configured.

These months later,
she is beginning
to feel her body again,
like tiny desert flowers
opening

2001

SOMEONE

for my friends and family

I am outside in the garden cutting rosemary
stalks. I rinse them under the front porch tap.
A tiny snail falls on the stoop, curls in a ball.
Don't worry, snail, I say out loud, and carry her,
place her with care, back on the stalk

2001

In the First Years of the Twenty-First Century

In 2000, one in 8 women in the U.S. will develop breast cancer
in their lifetime, compared with one in 11 in 1983.

— National Cancer Institute, 2001

Her left breast, it is discovered, has been manufacturing sub-standard cells
in the basement at night, and with sweatshop labor, at that. The doors
have been locked and production revved up. She could not hear
the clank and commotion of speeded-up cell-making. Over the years,
to produce inferior cells, canisters of pesticides have been stashed
under the stairs, scraped from grapes and strawberries and every grain
and vegetable and fruit she's ever eaten. Toxins excreted from work-overload
stress have been meticulously collected and stored in bowls with heavy lids.
Basement shelves become over-stocked, and the hands of timeclocks whirr
out of control. Finally, cell-workers organize and strike, call in the press.
Women in breasts all over the world read about it over coffee in the morning
paper, pack their bags, fly to the United Women's Hall, gather to strategize.
It is decided. The doors of her breasts, then of all breasts are unlocked,
cell-laborers are released and invited in for tea. They are provided with jobs
documenting their stories about sub-standard cell-making. At last, we have
the answer to how breast cancer cells are constructed. Pesticides are banished
from food, and as of noon that day, all supply lines to work stress toxins
are cut. It is a day of jubilation. In cities all over the world, mammogram
machines, now obsolete, are piled as public monuments. And in the vise
that once crushed our breasts, are the testicles of chemical company profiteers.

2001

Aftermath, September 11, 2001

In the aftermath of the attack on the World Trade Towers
and the Pentagon, and the death of 3,000 of our sisters and
brothers, words left me. I wrote just the first few lines of this
poem, read it at a peace vigil a few days later. With our bombing
of Afghanistan and no news of Afghani casualties, I searched
for the math, the numbers of dead caused by our foreign policies.
It was a time of silence, weeks of reading and listening and learning.

"We are more powerful out of the flesh than in."

— Lucille Clifton

I.
Where am I when two hijacked planes hit
the twin towers of the World Trade Center?
Way out here on the west coast, inside the
television, finding it hard to breathe in concrete
dust, and as the hours grow and the rubble
grows and the dead grow, I am down
on my knees, scrubbing the kitchen floor

In New York, an attorney runs down eighty flights
of tower stairs, through fallen pilings, steel swords,
shards of glass. Concrete dust burns his eyes. *Keep your damn war
over there*, he says, *this is not my war*

II.
Not my war, and I'm inside the television, the
murdered dead are everywhere, the walls are peeling
and I am an emergency room nurse again, doing triage,
counting the dead, only this time, I am listening to their voices
erupting like small gas leaks, they are talking to each other, the dead,
across walls, across language, *we are more powerful out of the flesh
than in* they are saying, talking to each other, counting

I am inside the tunnel of voices inside the television.
More than concrete walls are falling, the pipelines
are open, news plugged up for years, a river flooding the floor,
not my war, the dead dragging their lives behind them
more powerful the dead from the Trade Towers, from the
Pentagon, from a field in Pennsylvania, talking
to the dead coming in from Iraq, the West Bank,
Tel Aviv, from Guatemala, El Salvador – even my own
murdered dead from Seredna, Russia, from Lodz,
in Poland, *enough*, they are saying, this is not my war

Voices calling home from the skies of New York,
counting themselves, *three thousand of us sliding*,
and through cables underwater Iraqi voices
calling, counting, *one million of us dead, and
5,000 more dying each month, your extinguishing
sanctions*, the dead, their voices, how many from Gaza,
the West Bank, from Tel Aviv, Jerusalem, they are
counting the bullets *made in Pennsylvania*, not my war

Voices from Chile, counting, marking each others' brows,
nights, the CIA-backed coup *we are more than whispers* of
the democratically-elected Allende government *we are
30,000 dead people and we are hungry*, not my war, voices
from the seething hills of El Salvador, U.S.-backed death squads
fill the eyes of El Mozote *we are 70,000 people*. Voices, erupting
from the blood hills of Nicaragua, down the pipelines from
U.S.-sponsored contra wars, *we are 30,000 dead*. Not my war,
in Guatemala *we are 150,000 killed and 50,000 disappeared*
in the 1954 CIA-sponsored-fruit-company coup; not
my war, *two million of us* killed in Vietnam; and *200,000
of us dead* in Hiroshima and Nagasaki, the cries
Enola Gay and Fat Boy couldn't hear

Not my war, *we are voices lost* in the U.S.- backed
house in Saudi Arabia, the apartheid regime
in South Africa, Suharto's dictatorship in Indonesia,
Marcos in the Philippines, and Israel's occupations
of Lebanon, the Golan Heights, Gaza.

Not my war, in the name of 'national interests,'
in the name of oil and coffee and guns and fruit,
in whose interests, the dead are saying, *your leaders*
have trained death squads, assassinated politicians,
not my war, *treated us as entirely expendable*

III.
Not my war that our foreign policy,
that makes our country a target of terrorism,
is a mirror to our domestic policy —
not my war, expendable, that we put in prison
one in four African American youths,
expendable, that we deny health care
to 43 million people, expendable, that we cut
women cut children from welfare and don't
track what happens to those who don't find jobs,
expendable, that we ignore three million
homeless people who live on the streets
and don't count them among the unemployed,

expendable, that we deny education
to how many million youths, not my war
that, in the aftermath of the Trade Towers, we steal
billions, bloodlet their health and education and
shelter, use it for fighter planes and bombs and
missile defense, not my war that, in the aftermath,
we kidnap the love pouring out between us, spill it
into flags and guns in service to the so-called war

Where am I when two hijacked planes hit
the twin towers of the World Trade Center?
Way out here on the west coast, inside the television,

and I know why I don't know these stories, not flashed
over and over on the screens, I know in which rooms
in which cities the decisions, *expendable,* were made
to censor how many killings from the news, I know
the names of our arms dealers and oil dealers and fruit
dealers, making a killing from these killings

You who sit around tables in those rooms, you who make
the decisions to go to war, the blood will not disappear.
The cries do not go away. Years of wandering underground,
your dead have found you, I have found you.

I am Lana Weisman from Seredna killed, *I am Etta
Weisman from Lodz* killed. *I am Menachem Adlersberg
from Chernovitz* killed. We are told these dead
are not related. It has taken all of their selves
to bring me to this moment. And we are just one river.

2001

THE BREASTED GOD

" . . . (T)he name of God can be shifted. God tells that very thing to Moses at the burning bush: that God was known to Moses' ancestors as El Shadie, the Breasted God, but that now God will be known as YHVH. If that switch from female energy was necessary at that period, then any name suggesting maleness may need to be abandoned in this period."

— Rabbi Michael Lerner, *Jewish Renewal*

After two millennia, the Breasted God returned
and wouldn't you know it, artists set to work
immediately, and crosses and stars of David
became breasts **oo** or **8** the shape of infinity signs.

And She sent out the message in one thousand
and seventy languages: *We're here forever so clean up
and come over. I'm inviting the whole family in for tea.*

So I went. We all went. You could hardly
get in the door. Everyone I've ever loved
was there. And so was everyone I've known
and heard about, and all of you I had yet to know.

Well, first off, She served tea. I mean, She Herself
served it. And She had all our favorite teas,
from each of our families' tea bins, *Of course,
why wouldn't I,* She said, and sat down. *So tell me.*

She wanted to hear our stories. She opened Her desk,
turned on Her computer and its Translation Program,
the one with the built-in speakers so we could all
understand each other, and as we talked, She took notes.

I mean, *She* took notes. Any other place, an assistant
would've taken notes. *I'm going to write down all
that You tell me, and then I'll read it back to You
so You can tell me if I've heard You right.*

Sounded like She really wanted to hear, alright,
and what's more She was writing it down.
It's up to You how you do this.

Well, no surprise, we couldn't agree on
how to do it. We soon realized that in Her house
no one had any more power than She did or
each other, so we just did it, told our stories.
One at a time.

It was like a Grand Intervention.
Of course that's how it was.
How could it be any other way?
We all knew what a muck we'd made of things.

And here's another thing: in Her house,
we discovered that what we all had in common,
everyone of us, was a fine-tuned Baloney Factor Meter.
And we used it. We were at that place where enough was enough.

So we sat there with this large I mean large family
and told each other our exact experiences. That was tough.
But we were in Her house and we felt emboldened by the group.
We talked, we heard, we used The Meter.

And it went on into the night and next day and next night and years
and we talked and listened and metered. And there rose in the room
a kind of centrifugal caring. Each word carried it.

And She took down each of our stories and the group's responses
and read it all back to us and we listened and we looked at each
other. Hard.

We knew so much about each other, that by then we *were* a family.
It was clear how we had hurt each other, how we loved each other,
where we had failed, where we had gotten it right.

And at last She said, *So go home and clean up what You now know*
and invite me to come visit. I will sit in Your kitchens next time,
see Your stories for myself. And then I will tell You mine.

2002

91

We created a global peace movement. To protest
the war on Iraq, ten million people marched
on seven continents on the same weekend.
Feb. 15, 2003

E-mails spinning the globe
please forward forward please
where to gather which bus what
time what day what troops
deployed what missiles
loaded onto which planes,
please sign please forward

Like the e-mails spinning
for weeks before we march,
we march a mass wave
of ten million we fill the streets
the air the airwaves whirling
the world with *no to war*

In San Francisco, Sao Paulo,
and London, in Bombay, in
Buenos Aires, Barcelona, Berne,
in Damascus, in Melbourne,
Montevideo, Toronto

and Tel Aviv, in Cairo,
Capetown and Hong Kong,
in Antarctica and Paris, in
Prague and New York, Jakarta
and Ramallah, in Rome, in
Mexico City, in Stuttgart, Taiwan

Johannesburg, Berlin, Andalucia
and Dublin, in Los Angeles,
in Leipzig, in La Paz, in East
Lansing, Madrid and Amsterdam,
Rio de Janeiro, in Santiago,
Sacramento, Santa Cruz

"They will tell you that these are the biggest anti-war
demonstrations since the sixties. No. These are the
biggest anti-war demonstrations in the history of the world."

— Bettina Aptheker, historian, Feb. 15, 2003

In the Bleakest Days

"In WWI, the ratio of military personnel killed to civilians was 8:1.
In WWII, it was 1:1. In the many smaller wars since 1945, the ratio has been 1:8.
This means that the victims of wars have changed: the great majority being civilians;
they are mainly women, children, and the elderly."

—Anne Llewellyn Barstow, *War's Dirty Secret*, 2000

U.S. bombardiers
are dropping bombs. Ordnances.
They fall on flesh, they

tear open the skulls
of women and men rushing
for shelter, they empty

the faces of children,
crush bodies carrying the
small lives of people

like us. It takes five
U.S. soldiers to lift
one bomb from its carrier

to the plane. Calculate
the tonnage dropped in our name

March 2003

EVOLUTION

The cry we hear may be the pain we feel,
may yet be that of birth.

— Starhawk

This could be the day when love
becomes the currency, minted
in coins and bills and bonds.
Imagine it: love, the currency,
forged in the mold of lifelong friends.
This is the day when peace
comes, when arms dealers
stop building guns and tanks,
melt steel instead into soup
pots and bicycles.
This is the day when physicists
who designed 'smart' bombs, build
hands instead for the paralyzed.
When military bases around the world
close down, and schools that teach peace
replace them. This is the day
when leaders put away their
speeches, transform their push
for power, go home to play on
the floor with their children.
This is the day when bread and fruit
fill plates in every home. When
all people, at last, are equal,
with banks of love to back them.

2003

This is a book that took more than ten years to write. Actually, two of the poems were written in the 80s, expanding the circumference of the book. It was when Edwin Meese, the then-attorney general, said in 1984, "There is no hunger in America," and then a Presidential Task Force followed with, "There is no documentable evidence of rampant hunger in our country," that I first catapulted myself into writing social action poems. I called my friend Kira Carrillo Corser, a photographer, and asked her if she wanted to join me in documenting what we knew to be true – that so many people in our San Diego neighborhoods were making the streets their home. She did and we did an exhibition that brought their voices and faces to galleries and state capital buildings, lodged them centrally in the public discussion. And for the next decade, we went on to do three more exhibitions and books, these in response to the increasing millions without health care.

For years, when friends asked me why I did this work, I didn't really have an answer, other than I felt compelled, somehow, to do it. I came to understand it in glimpses. I had been married for twenty years to a Holocaust survivor. His family used to tell me that they couldn't have survived if people who were not Jews hadn't helped them at some point along the way. And that stayed with me. So did these questions: if I had lived in Europe at that time, as a Jew, would I have known enough to get out early, when it was still possible? Or would I have denied it, like my great-aunts did? Or, if I were not a Jew, would I have helped someone who was? And the question here for me today: what may or may not be happening to me that I have to stand up for?

Another glimpse: in 1991, I was walking in Balboa Park in San Diego in a protest march against the Gulf War, the time of yellow ribbons and a nation constructed to war. I was carrying a sign: "Be A Matriot: Support Education." I can remember being spit on.

Another glimpse around that time, one behind inventing the word "matriot." I was born and grew up in Montreal, was an emergency room nurse, lived there for many years before moving to the U.S. The health care system in Canada is not perfect, but it is a compassionate one, and not linked to a job. If you're sick, you get care. Living in the U.S., coming to realize the-then 37 million people without health insurance, and the announcement of our defense industry designing a 'patriot' missile, such was the cauldron for my re-envisioning what 'love of country' meant to me.

I also think of the physicist at my dinner table one night during that war, telling me that he designed 'smart' bombs. I asked him what he would do with this technology if he were using it for peaceful means. "I would use it to build hands," he said, "for people who are paralyzed." We may not know what our world can alternatively be like, but this surely gave me a glimpse of how little we are asking for.

Speaking of bombs and guns and killing, here's another Canadianism: the first gun I saw up close was when I was thirty-three years old. I was with friends, sitting around a dinner table, and they were talking guns. It was in the mid-70s and I had just moved to the U.S. from Canada. I said to my host, seated to my left, that I'd never seen a gun up close. "Are you kidding?" he said. "Wait here." And he went to his bedroom, brought back a handgun, placed it on the white tablecloth beside my fork. Metal. The size of my hand. Loaded.

How can I describe what this felt like for me? Someone from Canada, where few young women and men went into the military, a country where the military was a small part of the national budget, where guns and rifles and bullets were not part of my everyday life. That he had it in his house, in his bedroom, beside who knows what, his underwear, his pillow, where he and his wife slept, where tenderness and vulnerability and trust wrap them together in the dark. And this metal thing, smelling of death beside them in the night.

We are a country of guns and killing. We are the biggest exporter of arms in the world. It doesn't have to be like this.

On June 14, 2000, I was diagnosed with breast cancer. Needless to say, the poems came with difficulty, a few lines at a time. A few months later, I remember standing under pine trees waiting for a doctor's appointment, and the focus of the book became clear. For years, I had been writing poems in response to what I believe to be the inhumanity of our profit-driven culture. And now this disregard had landed on my doorstep. The estrogen pills I had taken that had caused the cancer, the pesticides on the food I had eaten that had caused the cancer, the work overdrive stress that had compromised my immune system and caused the cancer. What had been happening to me — my "left breast... manufactur-ing sub-standard cells/in the basement at night"— and I hadn't known it, was what I had been standing up for, for years. For years, I had been writing matriot poems.

And then Sept. 11, 2001. The same disregard that places profits before health in the boardrooms of chemical companies or health care companies is the same disregard that drives our foreign policies to deplete resources of countries around the world, that sup-ports and trains armies of dictators to keep this greed in place, that produces fanaticism, and that makes the U.S. a target of terrorism. It doesn't have to be like this.

What I wish for is that those who read this book will bring the matriot concept and word into their everyday lives and conversations, and apply its definition. For example, the president has declared September 11th to be "Patriot" Day. Given the definition, what would a "Matriot" Day look like? And given the "Patriot" Act that attacks our civil liber-ties in the name of national defense, what would a Matriot Act establish in its name?

I am reading my poems over one last time before sending them to the publisher, read-ing them from the beginning, poem by poem, walking into the moments along the path, stepping back eighteen years, ten, six... I know this woman I have walked back to meet. The one whose voice sometimes crackles the air. And the earlier voice, so outraged. Per-haps the outrage takes over a few poems at times, I am thinking. I reach to snatch these poems out of the collection and 'fix' them. Or take them out entirely, I say to myself, here so many years later, supposedly knowing more, seeing more. But I resist, I resist. The poems will stay as they were written in their time, the woman, following "the risings under her skin." Risings, throughout the book, her poems lodged in the political, and the per-sonal interrupting, and there it is, on her own doorstep. I am the woman I was. I have her by the arm. And I am also the woman I will be.

Frances Payne Adler, 2003

"A Call to Arms and Breast Cancer" (page 25).

Poet Audre Lorde died in 1992 after 15 years of living with breast and liver cancer.

"What possible choices do most of us have in the air we breathe and the water we must drink?"
Source: Audre Lorde. *A Burst of Light*. (Ithaca, New York: Firebrand Books, 1988), 120.

"Women with the highest exposure to the pesticide DDT, have four times the breast cancer risk."
Source: Mary S. Wolff, Ph.D., et al. "Blood Levels of Organochlorine Residue and Risk of Breast Cancer." *Journal of the National Cancer Institute* 1993; 85:648-652.

"Our data do not support the hypothesis that exposure to DDT and PCBs increases the risk of breast cancer."
Source: "Plasma Organochlorine Levels and the Risk of Breast Cancer." David J. Hunter, M.B., B.S., Susan E. Hankinson, Sc.D., Francine Laden, S.M., Graham A. Colditz, M.B., B.S., JoAnn E. Manson, M.D., Walter C. Willett, M.D., Frank E. Speizer, M.D., and Mary S. Wolff, Ph.D. *New England Journal of Medicine* (Oct. 30, 1997), Number 18.

"Chlordane" (page 26).

"Prevention of breast cancer may require intervention at an early age . . ."

". . . DDT belongs to a class of organochlorines that includes a number of other pesticides — chlordane, hexachlorobenzene, benzene hexachloride (aka lindane), for example — and halogenated biphenyls (polychlorinated biphenyls or PCBs)."
Source: Mary S. Wolff, PhD., "Pesticides — How Research Has Succeeded and Failed in Informing Policy: DDT and the Link to Breast Cancer." *Environmental Health Perspectives*. 103. (Suppl 6): 87–91 (1995).

"Turkey Vulture Venture" (page 27).
"Comparison of Factory Prices of Prescription Drugs in U.S. and Canada, 1991."
Source: United States General Accounting Office. "Prescription Drugs: Companies Typically Charge More in the U.S. Than in Canada." *Report to the Chairman, Subcommittee on Health and the Environment, Committee on Energy and Commerce, House of Representatives* (Washington, D.C. 1991).

"Emergency Room, U.S.A." and "The Great Lie" (pages 29 and 30).

National estimates of people without health insurance, 1990s to present:

1993: Number of people in the U.S. with no health insurance in 1993: 37 million.
Source: Families U.S.A, a health care consumer group.

1998: "Americans without health insurance jumps to 43.2 million despite booming economy, 1998."
Source: Universal Health Care Action Network (UHCAN) Website, http://www.uhcan.org, quoting from Physicians for a National Health Program. http://www.pnhp.org.

2001-02: "74.7 million Americans under 65 years of age — almost one out of three — were uninsured at some point during 2001–2002 . . . Working families are increasingly at risk of becoming uninsured — whether due to a pink slip from a job, unaffordable cost increases, or cutbacks in employer and public health coverage."
Source: Ron Pollack, Families U.S.A. (March 5, 2003). http://www.familiesusa.org.

"Los Desaparecidos" (page 31).

National estimates of homelessness, 1980s to present:

Late 1980s: "The number of adults experiencing homelessness was between 4 and 8 million at some point in the latter half of the 1980s . . . When the number of children is added, the range is 4.95 to 9.32 million . . . "
Source: Mary Ellen Hombs citing a 1994 government report, "Priority Home! The Federal Plan to Break the Cycle of Homelessness" in *American Homelessness: A Reference Handbook.* Santa Barbara, CA: Contemporary World Issues, ABC-CLIO. Third Edition (2001).

1996: "Nationally . . . between 2.3 and 3.5 million individuals . . . were homeless over the course of a year."
Source: Heidi Sommer, citing a 1996 Urban Institute Study in *Homelessness in Urban America: A Review of the Literature.* Berkeley, CA: Institute of Government Studies Press. 2001. http://urbanpolicy.berkeley.edu/pdf/briefbook.pdf or Urban Institute. *A New Look at Homelessness in America* (Feb. 01, 2000). Washington, D.C.: Urban Institute. http://www.urban.org.

2002: "Over the past year, over three and a half million people were homeless. Thirty-nine percent are children."
Source: National Coalition for the Homeless, Washington D.C. http://nationalhomeless.org.

"Los Desaparecidos" *Cont'd*

2002: "As housing costs continued to rise faster than incomes and the national economy remained weak, requests for emergency food assistance increased an average of 19 percent over the past year, according to a 25-city survey in 2002, released by the U.S. Conference of Mayors . . . The survey finds that 48 percent of those requesting emergency food assistance were members of families with children and that 38 percent of adults requesting such assistance were employed."
    Source: Washington, D.C: U.S. Conference of Mayors (Dec. 18, 2002). http://usmayors.org/uscm/news/press_releases/documents/hunger_121802.asp.

"In the First Years of the Twenty-First Century" (page 85).

In 2000, one in 8 women in the U.S. will develop breast cancer in their lifetime, compared with one in 11 in 1983.
    Source: National Cancer Institute, 2001, Bethesda, MD. http://seer.cancer.gov.

"Aftermath, September 11, 2001" (page86).

Sources:

Chile:
    Parenti, Michael. "The Mean Methods of Imperialism." *The Sword and the Dollar: Imperialism, Revolution, and the Arms Race* (New York: St. Martin's Press, 1989), 57.

El Salvador:
    Parenti, Michael. "Imperialism Domination Updated." *Against Empire* (San Francisco: City Lights Books, 1995), 25.

Guatemala:
    Brogan, Patrick. *The Fighting That Never Stopped: A Comprehensive Guide to World Conflict Since 1945* (New York: Vintage, 1990), 427.

    Chomsky, Noam. "U.S. and the World." *The Chomsky Reader* (New York: Pantheon, 1987), 328–329.

    Galeano, Eduardo. "Theater of Good and Evil." *The Progressive* (Madison, WI. Nov. 2001), 15.

Hiroshima, Nagasaki:

 A-Bomb WWW Museum, http://www.csi.ad.jp/ABOMB

Iraq:

 Clark, Ramsey. Former U.S. Attorney General, Letter to Ambassador and Foreign Minister of each member of the U.N. Security Council and U.N. General Assembly (Dec. 11, 2001). http://www. iacenter.org

 Niva, Steve. "Understanding Middle Eastern Sources of Violence Against The United States." Professor, International Politics and Middle Eastern Studies, Evergreen State College, Tacoma, Washington (Sept. 21, 2001).

New York, Washington, D.C., Pennsylvania:

 Milne, Seumas. "The Innocent Dead in a Coward's War." *Guardian,* quoting Marc Herold, Professor of Economics. University of New Hampshire (Dec. 20, 2001).

 Talbot, Margaret. "Order of Magnitude." *New York Times Magazine* (New York. Dec. 30, 2001).

Nicaragua:

 Chomsky, Noam. "The Decline of the Democratic Ideal." *Deterring Democracy* (London: Verso, 1991), 322.

Vietnam:

 Baritz, Loren. *Backfire: A History of How American Culture Led Us into Vietnam and Made Us Fight the Way We Did* (New York: William Morrow, 1985), 344.

 Parenti, Michael. *The Sword and the Dollar: Imperialism, Revolution, and the Arms Race* (New York: St. Martin's Press, 1989), 44.

ABOUT THE AUTHOR

Frances Payne Adler is the author of four previous books: *Raising The Tents* (Calyx Books, 1993), a collection of poems, and three collaborative poetry-photography books with photographer Kira Carrillo Corser: *When The Bough Breaks: Pregnancy and The Legacy of Addiction* (NewSage Press, 1993), *Struggle To Be Borne* (San Diego State University Press, 1987), and *Home Street Home* (Red Cross, 1984). Adler and Corser have four social action art exhibitions that have traveled the country, showing in galleries, universities, and state capitol buildings. Their most recent exhibition, "A Matriot's Dream: Health Care For All," showed on Capitol Hill in the Cannon Building in Washington, D.C., is on permanent loan to the Universal Health Care Action Network, and can be viewed on-line at www.matriot.org.

Adler's poems and prose have appeared in *Poetry International, Women's Review of Books, The Progressive, Ms. Magazine, Calyx, Fiction International, Exquisite Corpse, Bridges, Centennial Review,* and *Blood To Remember: American Poets on the Holocaust,* among others.

Her awards include a California State Senate Award for Artistic and Social Collaboration, a National Endowment for the Arts Regional Award, a Margaret Sanger Award, and a Helene Wurlitzer Foundation Award. She was a Western States Book Award finalist for *Raising The Tents.*

Adler is the Director of the Creative Writing and Social Action Program at California State University Monterey Bay.